CHICAGO TRIBUNE TOWER

HOME LIFE INSURANCE BUILDING

SEARS TOWER

EMPIRE STATE BUILDING

CHRYSLER BUILDING

WORLD TRADE CENTER

ONE CANADA SQUARE
London, England ●

Chicago, IL ●

New York City, NY ●

TRANSAMERICA PYRAMID
San Francisco, CA
●

● **LOS ANGELES CITY HALL**
Los Angeles, CA

SEAGRAM BUILDING

FLATIRON BUILDING

NY LIFE INSURANCE COMPANY

GOVERNMENT TOWERS
● Brasilia, Brazil

PALACE OF CULTURE
● Warsaw, Poland

NATIONAL COMMERCE BANK
Jeddah, Saudi Arabia ●

CHICAGO BEACH TOWER HOTEL
● Dubai, United Arab Emirates

PENTRONAS TOWERS
Kuala Lumpur, Malaysia ●

BANK OF CHINA

CENTRAL PLAZA

Hong Kong, China ●

LANDMARK TOWER
Yokohama, Japan ●

SKY CITY 1000
Tokyo, Japan

CARLTON CENTRE
● Johannesburg, South Africa

RIALTO TOWER
Melbourne, Australia ●

INTO THE SKY

by Ryan Ann Hunter

illustrated by
Edward Miller

SCHOLASTIC INC.

New York Toronto London Auckland Sydney
Mexico City New Delhi Hong Kong

Thanks, Dan, for reminding me to stand tall —E. G. M.

For Neil, Jack, Jared, Derek, and Kate —P. D. G.

To my niece Lauren Ann Sasso —E. M.

ISBN 0-439-16338-2

Text copyright © 1998 by Pamela D. Greenwood and Elizabeth G. Macalaster.
Illustrations copyright © 1999 by Edward Miller III. All rights reserved.
Published by Scholastic Inc., 555 Broadway, New York, NY 10012,
by arrangement with Holiday House, Inc.
SCHOLASTIC and associated logos are trademarks and/or registered trademarks of Scholastic Inc.

12 11 10 9 8 7 6 5 4 3 2 1   0 1 2 3 4 5/0

Printed in the U.S.A.   24

First Scholastic printing, January 2000

The authors would like to thank Dr. Lynn S. Beedle of the Council on Tall Buildings and Urban Habitat at Lehigh University for his assistance.

The illustrator would like to thank Yasunaga Tatsumi of the Takenaka Corporation and Wm. Scott Field, AIA, President of The Parkinson Archives.

Skyscrapers reach right into the sky. Some days, the tops of the tallest ones are hidden in clouds.

The first skyscraper was built about 100 years ago. A huge fire had destroyed a lot of buildings in Chicago. People needed new ones. Architects had new things to make taller buildings possible, like steel and safety elevators. Though the **Home Insurance Building** was only 10 stories high, it was a start.

It wasn't long before skycrapers were 20 or 30 or 40 stories high. Then, the **Empire State Building** went higher than 100 stories. But the tallest buildings of the 20th century are the **Petronas Towers** in Malaysia.

You could never build a structure of bricks or stone so tall. The weight of each floor and wall sitting on top of the others would make it collapse.

Flatiron Building   **Chicago Tribune Tower**   **New York Life Insurance Company**

Empire State Building

Petronas Towers

A skyscraper is built in a different way. A **frame** is made from steel or concrete. **Columns** go up and down. **Beams** go across. The frame holds the building up, just like your skeleton holds you up.

Engineers use wind tunnels to test models of skyscrapers. The frames have to withstand strong gusts.

There's a big part of the skyscraper you don't see. Before the frame goes up, backhoes dig a huge hole for the **foundation**. It can go four or more floors deep.

KEEP
OUT

POST
NO
BILLS

Sometimes steel **pilings** are hammered down to solid rock. They are bolted to the columns and hold the skyscraper in place like roots hold a tree.

In Texas, where the solid rock is too far down, skyscrapers are built on thick slabs of concrete.

In Los Angeles, engineers are putting rubber pads under the old City Hall to hold it steady and keep it from collapsing when earthquakes shake the ground.

It takes a very large team of people to put a skyscraper up. Cranes are used to lift the steel beams. Ironworkers wrestle the beams in place. They tighten thousands of bolts. They weld the pieces together.

When the ironworkers reach the top, they raise a fir tree or a flag into the sky, just like mountain climbers when they reach the top of a new peak.

A few floors below, other workers hang wall and window sections almost like curtains. They install pipes and wires. They paint and decorate the rooms.

Finally, they reach the top floor too, and the building is done.

PARKING

HOTEL

RESTAURANT

HOTEL

THEATER

ROYAL THEATER

THEATER

RESTAURANT

Skyscrapers are busy places, full of thousands and thousands of people in offices, restaurants and stores, apartments and hotel rooms.

Taller skyscrapers are being designed all the time. In Japan, architects have a model for **Sky City 1000**. It would be 196 floors tall. Triple-decker elevators would whisk people up and down.

People in some cities don't want new skyscrapers to cast shadows on other buildings, or parks.

But people still dream about skyscrapers as tall as mountains.
Who knows how high they could go?

CHICAGO TRIBUNE TOWER

HOME LIFE INSURANCE BUILDING

SEARS TOWER

Chicago, IL ●

EMPIRE STATE BUILDING

CHRYSLER BUILDING

WORLD TRADE CENTER

New York City, NY ●

TRANSAMERICA PYRAMID
San Francisco, CA
●

ONE CANADA SQUARE
London, England ●

● **LOS ANGELES CITY HALL**
Los Angeles, CA

SEAGRAM BUILDING

FLATIRON BUILDING

NY LIFE INSURANCE COMPANY

GOVERNMENT TOWERS
● Brasilia, Brazil

PALACE OF CULTURE
● Warsaw, Poland

ATIONAL COMMERCE BANK
Jeddah, Saudi Arabia ●

CHICAGO BEACH TOWER HOTEL
● Dubai, United Arab Emirates

PENTRONAS TOWERS
Kuala Lumpur, Malaysia ●

BANK OF CHINA

CENTRAL PLAZA

● Hong Kong, China

LANDMARK TOWER
Yokohama, Japan ●

SKY CITY 1000
Tokyo, Japan

CARLTON CENTRE
● Johannesburg, South Africa

RIALTO TOWER
Melbourne, Australia ●